Winterwood Poems

Winterwood Poems

LEE OLIVIER CLEGHORN

authorHOUSE®

AuthorHouse™
1663 Liberty Drive
Bloomington, IN 47403
www.authorhouse.com
Phone: 1-800-839-8640

First published by AuthorHouse   07/09/2011

ISBN: 978-1-4634-3274-4 (sc)
ISBN: 978-1-4634-3273-7 (dj)
ISBN: 978-1-4634-3272-0 (ebk)

Library of Congress Control Number: 2011911955

Printed in the United States of America

Table Of Contents

Index Of First Lines

My Home, My Harbor

My Home, My Harbor

My Home, My Harbor

Down the Tunneled Lane

Their lane was tree-tunneled long
   and curved one way,
   a slow arc
   as deliberate as their love:
A quiet pine needle passage
   running close into hut-thatched snugility,
The house at its open end tucked deep
   the hillside catching the sun
Facing away-- by their choice-- the dread,
   noised course of commerce.
It sat proudly high, gray, spare
   and beautiful--
Sucking warmth there, taking breath
Where that green lane turned
   gently into glory--

Happy were they secreted there
Surveying God's own Eden.

                                   September 4, 1986

3

My Home, My Harbor

Along with Spring

Yesterday
your poem arrived
to let me know
you understood my pain
and it has helped.

Today,
my eyes look out
in search of spring
or some small sign
of winter's end.
But misty February cold
brings silver greys and white
intruding further neutered days
into my wintered life. For now,
your poems are all I have
to warm me through 'til spring.
Last night's new snow
is powdered white
and rests in layered rifts
at fringes of our woods.

Elusive deer
escaped our Winterwood
this morn. Faint hoof-prints show
near scruffy grasses peeping through.

My Home, My Harbor

The pines,
with knify limbs askew
tremble in transparent coats.
They, like me, impatiently endure
new sentencing.
I am put off by them,
am surfeited by all this white,
this virgin snow, this cold,
and with this icy winter
lengthening...
I'm forced to stay indoors.

I seek reprieve
from its locked jaws
and look again for signs of spring.
I find it there where early bluebird scouts
nibble apple slices we have thrown,
and find it there beside our path
as one lone daffodil, celebrating self,
its perfect cheek delicate with ice,
breaks through its white prison,
spread green arms outstretched
to sing in yellow wonder
things to come.

Amid these little
subtle signs of spring,
again I search the road, the path, the drive
for more than fragile footprints in the snow:
some signs you might be coming, too,
along with spring.

February 10, 1988

5

My Home, My Harbor

The House That Didn't Belong

At first
The land resented
The intrusion of the house,
Being built as it was
On the side of the hill,
Once wooded and brushed
Where deer crossed and quail lived.
So the soil lay there slipping and sliding
With each rain, mumbling
Its displeasure with loosened
Clay and shifting sands.
Unsure. Threatened.
Its first claim being lost,
Giving sway to piers and beams
Imbedded here, there.

But then
The house went up,
Its builders conscious
All the while of
Valued trees and shrubs,
Of nesting down amid
Existing wooded site with sparing plan
To rest along its natural slant.
The grumbling soil at last gave in
Relented to the strange intrusion,
Made room for it and settled down
Contoured itself to gracefully accept
The newer presence on the land
Of this hill straddling stranger,
At last, at last
Even welcomed it
As friend.

November 1985

My Home, My Harbor

Leaving the City
for East Texas

The city shuns me.
Having turned its
Back on me,
Pretends the fault
Was mine.
Its cold concrete shoulders
Make hard pillows
Casting shadows
Over all once
Found beautiful.
Even as we flee
Its coldness
Pursues . . .
With long stretches
Of snaky arms
It reaches outward
To reclaim its lost past.
But we know
As the city knows:
All Roads Lead Away.

March 30, 1985

My Home, My Harbor

Leaves of Texas Autumn

There is a different color
To the air in autumn
A color bed of palette many hued
Laid down upon earths carpet
In the autumn
The golden leaves of autumn
Lead me home.

With every curve of path
And turn of pathway
A new surprising color hews its splendor
Each vibrant blotch of splatter
Leads me on
The gold and rusty leaves of autumn
Dance me home.

Each leaf a dancy swirl
Of quiet surrender
To life's repeated earthy twirl of time,
A crisis or a triumph of the seasons
In the autumn,
The gusty leaves of autumn
Drive me home.

October 10, 1985

First Place, Annual Awards December
1985 Rusk County Poetry Society. Pub-
lished 1986: Rusk County Poetry Society
Anthology of Poems "Sing Sesquicenten-
nial".

My Home, My Harbor

The House

The land slants downward
An angular slope
From where the house
Sits on the hill
At the top hugging
The earth
At the bottom flying
Out from it into space
Head and shoulders
Into the trees
Commanding attention.
My dream
Become my house
Becomes me
Cathecting it totally.
Those halls I walk
Those decks covered
Hold windows which
Look out critically
Upon the world
Through my own
Prejudiced eye
Liking what I see.

February 7, 1986

My Home, My Harbor

Her House

Her house held
Arched windows
Where multi-faceted mirrors
Hung facing the world.
Her private rooms
Proved mansioned
In her house,
Where all guests were welcome
And well fed...
But none too long.

February 1986

My Home, My Harbor

A New Found Friend

I've found a new friend in East Texas
I wander out to see her in the fall
A winding ribbon through the tresses
Of the Autumn leads the eyes
To feasts of nature in her hair.
The distant hills and valleys flowing outward
And up and down on either side of me
Clad in multi-colored beauty in the Autumn
A land of finery and elegance indeed.
Opened wide the arms of Mother Nature,
Captivating me with all her luring charms
Of eyelid and of hip rise and of dresses,
The golden-amber-russet of her hair.

Yes I've found a new friend in East Texas
In the country all around me she reclines
And a million of her brightly colored leafings
Fall like rusty wasted tendrils of her year.

November 9, 1985

My Home, My Harbor

My World

I spin outward
In ever widening
Circles into the universe
Where I Live. I spin
Creating my own
Galaxies, stair-tripping
Stars. Stone white
Star pads ascending
Ever higher
Lend me ascension ...
Make somehow that unknown
Sky trip bearable.
Where I fall or slip
Am brought back
To within the realm
Of sharp white possibility
Am knee jerked
Into proper space
To places nearer
My total intended
Picture of reality
In ever closing circles
Nearer Earth.

December 1, 1985

My Home, My Harbor

The Cranberry Dish

I am a servant on a stem,
Cranberry red but clear.
Should you ignore my burnished rim,
I shall become quite dear.

December 15, 1987

My Home, My Harbor

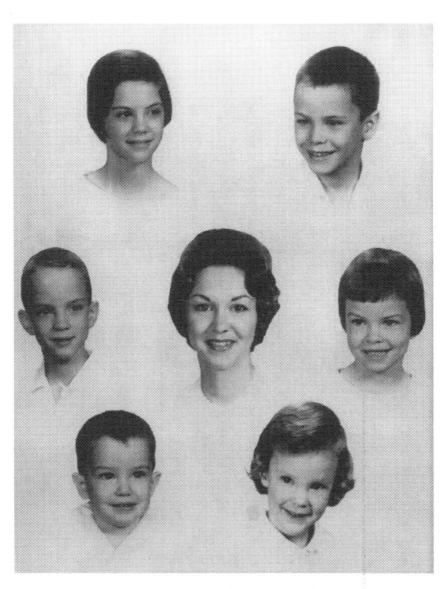

Childhood

Childhood

The Backyard War

We did some things when we were kids
For lack of something new.
For lack of newer plastic toys
We built our own and true.
We made slingshots and rubber guns
To play at cops and robbers
But the favorite of all, I like to recall,
Were the soldiers we made for the war.

Just me, my brothers Gene and Will
And Tommy Tuttle too.

Strong molded metal soldiers they were,
Painted red, brown-khaki and blue.
They carried guns with bayonets sharp.
They'd shoot you or stab you through
To die on some hot desert sand.
And talked of war in nations far
Right there in our backyard land.

Just me, my brothers Gene and Will
And Tommy Tuttle too.

See, you go through the back door
... After the porch...
Then through the screen door too,
Down three steps and into the yard
And you're in Timbuktu!
Where wars are fought!!
And I mean Wars!!!... with
Soldiers: French! Arabs! and Jews!

Just me, my brothers Gene and Will
And Tommy Tuttle too.

Childhood

If you stay awhile 'til the shooting starts
You'll see a war ensue
With soldiers on horseback fighting mad
With some combating hand to hand,
Some die with their boots on
Dying for valor... some
Dying go... barefoot,
But all in the backyard sand.

Just me, my brothers Gene and Will
And Tommy Tuttle too.

The sand's all laid out in valleys and dunes
(It's really just backyard dirt)
But with dugouts and foxholes and garrisons
Built for men in red-streaked brown-khaki suits.
With blood and guts and shoot-em-ups,
With rifles and pistols and sabers
And trickery, spying and plots
And guys on the battlefield crying.

Just me, my brothers Gene and Will
And Tommy Tuttle too.

For we were the Foreign Legion Men!
Had you been there you'd've been one too,
Fighting beside us hand to hand
With rifles and pistols and sabers.
You'd die with your boots on, dying for valor
or dying go... barefoot.
For it was the Foreign Legion War
Laid out in the backyard sand.

Just me, my brothers Gene and Will
And Tommy Tuttle too.

January 16, 1975

17

Childhood

Childhood Memories

Homemade scooters
And rubber guns,
The games of tag ...
And Betty Boop,
The hide-and-seek
And loop-the-loop.
The kick the can,
The bubble gum
And watermelons
In picnic sun.
Red Rover games
And tugs of war,
The "One-potato
Two-potato
Three-potato four".
The "Who's-at-bat?"
In sand lot ball
And "I have dibs
At marbles, y'all".
The summer showers
With the hose,
The lemonade stands,
The dolly clothes,
The skates ... the barn
The barnloft hay
The barefoot days
The "Milky Ways".
All these memories
Cherished dears ...
Precious from
My Childhood years.

September 17, 1986

18

Limericks

Limericks

There was a young Doc named Solis

Whose calling it was to police

Errant persons who choke

Their own lungs up with smoke

But without whom his career would decrease.

February 1981

There once was a programmer named Kevin

Whose computer was not really revvin'

When he entered his data

His program went splatta,

Now with more validation he delves in.

February 18, 1987

20

Nature

Nature

Nature

The Firefly

Night falls
And the firefly
Lights evenings dark spaces
Each brief beam, on, off, sudden night
Magic.

       August 1-13, 1987

Sun Child

Daybreak,
And the orange disk
Climbs up the horizon
Bright child climbing out from his crib
Of night...

       August 1-13, 1987

July

July,
Sun beating down
Bent hazy rays of days
Makes sweaty necks grow prickly heat
To scratch.

       August 1-13, 1987

Nature

Evening Lullaby

Chuck Will's
Widow flies from
Tree to tree to night cry
Me to sleep. But I hear her song
And weep.

August 1-13, 1987

Daybreak

Sunrise,
Morning's gold arms
Reach out to take in day,
Embrace it full and say goodbye
To night.

August 1-13, 1987

Nature

After a Heavy Rain

In the after rain quiet
Rain drops rivulet the window pane
Silently spinning water webs,
The only sound a soft drip of splatter
Falling from the wet trees outside
As they shed excesses on
   our porch roof.
Like mute showered statues
Longing to be dry again
Their water logged tresses droop
Toward the soggier earth
at their root feet.
Fresh-washed of dust,
Pine needles hold
A fresher piney scent.
The birds have it,
And they know it.
Before their feathers are dry
They are aperch in the still wet trees
Singing to the sun.

November 3, 1985

Nature

The Autumn Parade

In the autumn parade
The trees toss their hats
Into the air
Feathers, brims veils fly
Curly brims flirting
Like floating wings
Crests dancing
Twirls to sassy beat
Each rhythmic movement
A Millener's Heaven
This hat parade
A flame and russet
Of golden and berry
Which fly about madly
Until finally all hats
Are off and down.
All is still
And nothing is left
To the Autumn dance
Save the colorful quiet
Crazy-quilt of leaves
The after-parade confetti.

November 10, 1985

26

Nature

Before Birdsong

On the cheek of dawn

A blueness creeps out

Before the birds sing

Before they take to winging

It through

Unpredictable dayness

And orangeity comes,

Begins to persuade

Into yellow light,

Willing them to flight.

Like fragile light rays

Foretell sunrise:

Feathery, sweeping

Is a birdwing seen

Before birdsong.

January 28, 1986

Nature

Good Morning World

The Mockingbird this early morning sings

All the songs which God has given wings.

That bird puts his whole being into song,

A supreme example to the lagging throng.

He sings his songs as though to never stop,

Having perched himself in tallest tree, at top

To tell the world this morning nothing's wrong

Or, if there is, his song would make it right.

March 5, 1976

Nature

Haiku

Three Buzzards circling
Haystack burrow bare
Furry rabbit lying dead

                              February 26, 1987

Bluebirds scouting sites
Sun melts ice on barb wire fence
Nesting time down south

                              February 26, 1987

Midnight owl hooting
Silver moonbeams slice through sky
Fat orange pumpkin shines

                              February 28, 1987

Geese rest marshy pond
Warming green reeds sprouting new
Long, long trip ahead

                              March 1, 1987

Rye grass green knee high
Rains cut southwind blowing north
Soon is time to mow

                              March 1, 1987

Frog leap ripples pond
Lily pad a waterbed
Ride open lily

                              March 8, 1987

Nature

Rainbow arc to sky
Colored staircase to the clouds
Highway to heaven

February 6, 1987

Golden moon shines bright
Lonely cowboy sits his horse
Hear coyotes wail

August 29, 1987

Autumn Pine tree stands
Some green needles turning brown
Nature makes Christmas.

November 1, 1986

Icy tree limbs bare
Frozen branches crying
North winds blowing cold

November 25, 1986

At the foot of ice-clad
Mountain a brave blossom
Sings in perma-frost.

July 25, 1985

Nature

In My Chosen Wildness

Not in verdant gardens
Do I walk
With flowered borders
Set in rows
But brambled wilds,
With pine trees high
Protective to
The forest floor,
Littered needlebeds
For dens of deer
Between stump
And fallen log.
Tri-leveled woods
Walk I from here...
Beneath the dogwood
Wide palmetto fronds,
Wet natural ferns,
The wild wild rose...
Amid it all
In dappled light
I sense the breath of hare.
My flowers are
Uncultured ones which
Dress the forest edge
Like yellowed lace
Sewn on the hem of summer skirt
Spread wide
Upon green turf.
They grow from oranged rock
And speak of life which springs
From barren space,
Not fettered
Nor contained
And not set out
But free...
And so like me   June 11, 1987

Nature

March

March is a blowhard lion
Running rampant in the street
Roaring wide his angry growl
White mane flying in the sky.

March is a soft fluff of magician
Struck by mother natures wand
A greening, budding flagrance
Sprouting out of icy ground.

At once a king proclaiming dominance
And a wee lamb turning tail.

August 24, 1986

Nature

One Other Summer June like this

It took
Eternities of spring
To make one summer June
Like this

Giftings
From the gods who thought
To lure us into summer with
Such June

So hot
And green soaking wet
To hottest sun then
Pouring down

Again
In rain to lush my shrubs
With clear wet drops
In sheets

Sometimes
And at others often
In a slow soft pelt
Of wet.

I see
As I look backward
Through eternities of spring
One June,

Am awed
That future springs preceeding
June could never, ever
Make one

Other summer June like this.

June 24, 1987

33

Nature

Perfect Work of Patience

Outside
In the plum orchard
Across the space
Between me and its new
Verdancy, the largest thickly greened
Wild plum tree, dark trunk
Crooked by its wildness,
Teases me with new fruit.

I see
Through its flagrant
Eroticism, a bravado
Of globed fruitiness beckoning me
Toward round perfection.
My mouth waters my lips.

Each morning
I awake to stare
Across the distance,
My marveled eye measuring
Last night's pleasured growth.
An almost cadenced surge,
Fruit greenness tinged with pink
Next, a tiny spot of red.

Again
Another night
A spurt, a splurge, a raptured dewness.
This morning when I awake
I find to my delight
A fat red juicy reward
For my patience.

May 19, 1987

*First Place, Top Prize - Jackpot Award, East
Texas Fall Festival of Poetry 1987. Published:
Rusk County Poetry Society Yearbook, 1988.*

Nature

The Red Christmas Cactus

The red Christmas cactus
We set outdoors for summer
Returns to the house
For another December.

Refurbished, renourished
By care in spring sun ......
Outside it flourished
With rain, wind (or none).

Thus furnished by nature
And placed in a new pot
Sings out in red glory
As it enters the house.

To all who love Christmas
This flower will bear
Its Carmineate song
of Nativity near.

December 10, 1975

Nature

Re-Landscaping

If I had the
World to paint over
I'd have horizontal
Telephone poles
Or have them hidden
In the woods
Not have my eyes
Messed up with
Things I didn't
Want to see.
Too many signs
Traffic lights
Wires, Poles
Interrupt My view
Of what I think
The world should be.
I'd like to look
Out on a spread
Wide world
of flat and rise
Of trees that
Touch the skies
Yet have it all
Within my grasp
With naught to
Block my view
Without the poles
And wires strewn
Askew.
I'd have more room
To see the view
I'd have more
Space for you.

December 28, 1985

Nature

Vapor Trail

I draw his line
Across the sky
As surely and
As straightly
As did he whitely
Dip his trail in blue
When he flew
From star to star
Then down to moon
And back again.
Was then he flew
Laughing to the blue
Laughing that he knew
Knowing intimately
The winds, all four,
Slicing them clean...
Clearer than birdwing
Higher than their song
Could reach
Softer than an
Angel's kiss...
And true.

December 28, 1985

Nature

History, Current Events and Pop Culture

History, Current Events and Pop Culture

History, Current Events and Pop Culture

Donald Sams

Its dinnertime
And the evening news in on.
You can set your watch by his timing
But not your life by his philosophy
For if you do, you will lose.
He tells you not only what to think
He tells you how... at six o'clock
And what to think about what he thinks
All the time.
Always referring to "The President",
To "The Administration" or "The White House"
Never to "Our Country"
"We" or "This Beloved Land of Ours".
We begin to think, it's so often repeated,
Not only that he lacks these sentiments
But that his whole intent
Is meant to destroy:
What we really think,
What we believe,
What we know.
What a sad commentary
That a United States,
So united now as never before,
Is made to seem divided
By one frighteningly
Deranged
Commentator,
And the lies he tells.

September 2, 1987

41

Freedom

If those demanding freedom only knew
That liberty requires a selflessness,
And dedication to a cause is due
To country and to others - never less;

That freedom is a goal and not a loan,
Which if one were to pledge his all to get
But know no greater causes than his own
He would remain enslaved - a servant yet.

Then let him simply search it for itself
Not for reasons of motive or of creed
But solidly, steadfastly as a wealth
Of blessing and of virtue born to need -

A need not given nor bestowed but earned.
Freedom, through honor and through deed, is
learned.

August 29, 1985

The Gentle Aftermath of Challenger

After all the pieces have been retrieved
After the flotsam and jetsam have been laid out,
Examined, identified and partially pieced together
Jigsaw style over white sheets
Spread on polished hardwood floors
Having been handled perhaps gently, perhaps gingerly,
Being touched by more hands than any
Single rare archaeological find --
Puzzled and pondered over, patched,
Reseamed perhaps in strange new shapes,
The rubbish from our American Dream
Of space supremacy reinacted on a satin NASA floor --
After all the causes and cures have been discussed
One final jewel will be retrieved, retraced
Again and again
With soft white hands caressed, embraced.
There will be many little American babes
Reverently named: Christa.

January 30, 1986

History, Current Events and Pop Culture

The Yellow Rose Remembers

Do not mourn me
For my yellow skin,
Because I was a simple slave girl,
Or because I was ill used by men.
Though legend does not truly honor me,
My master, Morgan, trained me well.
He kept me from hunger
Until Santa Ana saw fit
To take me prisoner, and more...

But I knew where my loyalty lay...
When I sent the negro, Turner,
With messages to Houston,
I did it for Texas.
And history will tell:
Santa Ana was defeated
Because of his own
Uncontrolled passion
And I... I was freed.

August 29, 1987

44

Turnabout in the Evening News

I'd really like to zap the media
Who think they have us trapped inside a pen
Of desperation and defeat, to see
How they'd react on the receiving end.

It's painful to believe they would not care
Should we be perpetrators of their sin,
No matter what the gain be there,
Of lying always to our fellow men.

Would they in our deception find a fault
And finding it, keep letting _us_ tell lies?
If so, would they, like us, be slow to halt
The game of being always victimized?

It seems to me we'd all get clearer views
By never turning on the nightly news.

April 14, 1987

History, Current Events and Pop Culture

Introspection

Introspection

Introspection

Irresolute Spirit

An Irresolute Spirit
Is one which remains
Not satisfied with
The status quo
But walks in resolute halls
With soul unbent
By outer claims --
With inner soul content.
He strives to gather
Fruits of honor
And persists in duty
Considering time
Well spent
Which is spent in pressing on,
In weighing values
His duty to fulfill.
Being not dissuaded
By others' claims
But holding his own soul
Up to scrutiny
In the light,
He often finds himself in need
But wants to do what's right,
So makes amends.
If that be
Irresolute, I am.

September 1, 1986

Introspection

New Years Resolutions 1978-79

This year I make
For my Resolutions
A list of
Wills and Wont's
And Restitutions,
Of do's and dont's
And Absolutions,
Of charity work
For Institutions.
So it won't be hard
To remember later,
It's the same as my
Nineteen-Seventy-Eighter.

January 1, 1979

Introspection

Pain
She knew well
The strung pain
Having been doled
That certain cold hand
Of unsparing
Down counted
Unswept years
Knowing it intimately.
Those wasted, staired
Years through tunnels
Of unlit search
Were only as great
As her capacity for it.
She knew it totally
And once having tasted
The rancid tea
Knew then also
Well its dregs
And forever more
Looked into each cup
Before tasting.

November 27, 1985

Introspection

Preparation

For where eternal silence does prevail
Or darkness come
I practice to adjust to its domain,
In blackness walk and see,
In silence hear and be,
As to some future death
Or life I cannot plea.
Perhaps in blackeness
And in quiet both
I should foresee
A loneness . . .
Alone with only me.

September 20, 1978

Introspection

Private Searches

She tested them,
Weighing all three
Separately, each being
A distinct part
Of her Personal
Trinity. Perplexed,
She found each
Lacking in some
Mysterious way.
None could
Knowingly stand
Alone, so shadowless.
Tri-Crossed they stood
Intersecting her crux.

January 10, 1986

53

Introspection

Tears
From The Poet At Age 11

For happy tears
Of joy I will
To lay upon
My cheek I will
To linger there
And dry until
The day I die
But have them still.

No tears
Of sadness
Or of pain,
For they could
Never e'er remain
To wet my cheek
Like warm sweet rain.

For only tears
Of joy I will
To lay upon my cheek I will
To linger there
And dry until
The day I die
But have them still.

1940

Introspection

This Is My Life

From all the days I've tread
   this path called Life
I'd ask you choose at random -
   or at will - the best and worst;
Then give me your selection,
   last and first.
Forget not that I've lived
   a true existence
Nor forget it has been rich
   and full
With pain and pleasure and
   with mixed emotion,
With tenderness and tiredness
   - without skill,
And deem to me the day if
   not the hour
You found me shining glory
   - or transposed.
And I, from all my depths
   of years and days agree:
They are as one, inseparable,
   Beyond disparity.
They are Me.

May 5, 1971

55

Introspection

Who Is this Stranger?

My aging body aches
Cries for its lost youth
Through lips no longer
Smoothly firm
Old griefs now sit
In strange new linings
An unknown face
Looks back from
The mirror

Who is this Stranger there?

June 9, 1985

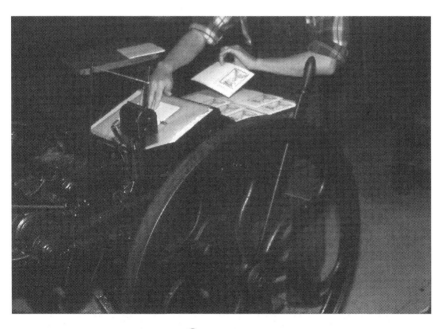

On Writing

On Writing

On Writing

Imagers of Jade

While waiting for the Muse
To grant me voice
On subjects I've endured
Yet have no choice,
I find myself a servant
In her land, a victim
Of her views, her plan.
Through eyes of mine
She sees into the ball
Of crystal clear - where
Mine, although not blind,
Are not as near
To sight
Not carried to the light
Of overseer nor x-rayed
Through for faults,
Or worth or clarity,
For with trifocaled,
  clouded eyes I see,
While hers, unfaded,
See with sharper imagers
  of Jade.

April 21, 1986

On Writing

The Lonely Line

How does one write of the
Pain of nothingness
For where there exists a void
Should exist nothing -
No pain - no feeling.
No cold or warmth
No beauty or joy, no music -
Poetry is All.
The word is Everything
And the Line is lonely.

January 14, 1974

On Writing

My Plate No Longer Empty, White

The word distilled
Drops soft upon my plate
And falling softly,
Gathers to it richness,
Rises from it sweeter now,
Your manna hoarded
For my winter's cold.

This was my Mother's winter too,
And therefore mine.
I broke from it
And wept.
While you were pacing rooms
Alone, I paced here in my own.
The gardener poet watched and knew:
She heard the cry, the break, the fall
And saw the long dry anguish
Fill my soul.

My white plate now
You fill with rendered heapings
Of your honest bread.
I take it in,
I taste it with my tongue.
My eager mind
Rapacious at your leavened gifts
Devours them,

On Writing

Your word upon honed word
Piled high, pyramided
On my humble shelf.
I take them up and run.

Before I leave my plate
Today, to look out
At the windowed sun
I say don't cry for me.
Like you in January chill
I see from my highest window
The tight white sheet has gone.

While we slept blanketed
From cold and fear
All around us Eden greened.
I see from heightened rooms
That garden, walked in late.
I see the poet, poet-gardener
And the bud
Along the flattened path.
I also see
Since you have come
The wintered walkway
Like my plate
No longer empty,
White.

April 3, 1987

On Writing

Poetry

It casts a singular glow
On everything I do-- this poetry--
Makes all my colors deeper shine
It takes my pen up
And with my hand
It Writes!
It Writes!

April 14, 1987

On Writing

Poet's Dilemma

Another day gone by
Without a book word being written
How long has it been . . .
A week, two weeks, a month, a year?

A lifetime!
My urging Spirit surges
Beyond the limits of my time.
Before the scratchings of my pen begin
I keep my lazy self in bed
While writing in my mind;
(Then so much lost that should've
    been written).
Foolish one! the book won't
    write itself -
Putting out its words, unbidden!
You must take your pen in hand
And let your surging spirit quicken.

January 5, 1975

On Writing

A Request of My Spirit

Poet
Wordsmith
Make me a word
Make it fit in
With the rest
Of my world
Make it a good one
One I can use
In utter tight
Moments
One I won't lose
In the ruts
Of my roads
Make it a winner
Keep it in tune
With my desires
For rhyme
And for scheme
And make it
To scan
One I can live with
Write with and love
Make it a winner
Sent from above
From whom but
My Wordsmith
My Poet
My Dove.

February 12, 1986

On Writing

The Room Poem

To walk through a poem as through a room
To be in the verse looking about,
Seeing, feeling, knowing
That is my poet-heart's desire.

July 21, 1985

On Writing

Vanity

What vanity is this   All unpredictable.
Which plagues my days,   It catches me asleep,
Pushes me to set on paper   Awake, or at my work.
Words I hope will
Live beyond my time?   It says: "Pickup up your pen
                                       And hold it so to paper.
It hides in corners   Start to write. Now that's the
Of my squared-off rooms,   way..."
Behind a table or a chair...   Audaciously it orders me,
Lurks and tries to catch me   And I obey.
Unaware, off-guard, to see   Then just before the punch line comes
                                       The muse is gone.
If I'll succumb. It plays
Light tricks or tucks itself   Oh, I see now, Vanity,
In shadows in the hall   Thy name is Poetry!
And celebrates the times
I'm taken by surprise.   August 16, 1987
With seeming mystery,
As in a cloud,
It comes and goes

67

On Writing

Writers Search

I am in that scary place
Where poets go
When no one else is watching,
Trying hard
In my diligent way
To tip the scales of justice
In favor of perfection. Ripping
Pain apart, robbing
Old graves, some better
Left to time. Crying diamond tears
Upon cold catafalques
Of wasted years,
Searching for purities,
Stars. Onenesses...
Looking even under rocks
For some new reality
To open itself like a
Perfect lily
Revealing all
To my eyes only.

August 3, 1985

First Place, Republic Bank Award, East Texas Fall Festival of Poetry, October 1985. Rusk County Poetry Society Yearbook, 1986, Touchstone, 1992

Spiritual

Spiritual

Spiritual

The Christmas Message

Its Christmas Eve and all around
The snow lies cold upon the ground.
Green wreaths are decked with red berries and bows
While indoors, hot drinks warm and fires glow.

Stockings hang empty, awaiting their fill
Children chatter and laugh as Children will:
Anticipating Santa, gifts, giving, and surprises
And the glorious world tomorrow's sun will arise in.

And glorious it is, this world that we live in
With Christmas still Christmas, Children still Children;
That in spite of our troublesome cares and fears
We manage to forget them 'til way past New Years.

We remain close and loving, unharried, content
Beyond expectation for this Christmas event
Unshadowed by doubts, frustration and gain,
Was this the Christmas Child's plaintive refrain

From His crib cold and dark, lit with heavenly love?
- Just so, in our hearts sings that enlightened dove:
So all on each Christmas are warm from within
Though the world from without be cold and grim.

December 21, 1971

Spiritual

Christmas Night

This Christmas Night
The house is lit
The fire warms
The tree stands green
The snow lies white
And cold and clean.

There is a frostiness
About the air
The stars shine bright
Through misty clouds
As unaware
As tree lights shine
Through angel hair.

There is a hush
About this night:
A calm. A peace.
Surcease from flight.
There lies the gift
Inside this night.
This Christmas night:
The Peace!
Surcease from flight.

December 11, 1975

Spiritual

Conversations with God

Once, in one of my quiet moments
I told God I loved him
And then asked him
To love me back.

He laughed,
Making me smile.

January 10, 1998

Spiritual

High Devil's Cross

Outsmart High Devil's Cross!
Sail brave pale sea
To Star. Sail free.
Dodge wayward inns
Set strong against the task,
Night blind to heaven's
   yawning cave.
Give light to errants
Way-feet caught
In molding clay.
A handshake, nod,
A smile, a tear awry,
A viselike grip
Of understanding eye,
Give all. A forehead rub
Of ashes from the Hand
May strike stray footprints
Water-dented from the Sand,
Lest time prove lost to
Hell's bent winding way
And heaven missed.
Unchart his course through mazes
Where False exit posts
Signed: "Satan-Lain"
Of Cross-wood made
Are ours to countersign.

October 17, 1977

74

Spiritual

His Birthday Cake in Green Pyramid

The tree of everlasting life
True symbol of His birth
Rises in green abundant pyramid
To a central star pointing heavenward.
More candles on His green cake
Than plausible for any other birthday ....
Trimmed in golden tinsel twinkling
In flashing clear white light ....
All golden and eternal in reflection,
A stunning display, In reverent array
But surely, surely lacking in some way.

Under this lighted cathedral
Man shelters his gifts
To be offered again this year
Again in His name, for His birthday.
Always, always trying, trying
But ever, ever failing, failing
To surpass, outdo, outshine ......
Forgetting, Oh, forgetting! His message:
He who gave the greatest gift of all
The gift of self to those one loves.

November 19, 1986

Spiritual

Immortal Spirit

Take flight
Fly to the clouds
At last
As on earth,
Your spirit looms
Greater than life
Greater than pain
Or earth-shackling
Mortal cares.
Take flight
For you have become
At last
At least
Angelic.

March 14, 1974

Spiritual

Joseph's Gift

I am Joseph
And this is my gift

The star shone brightly in the sky that night
One special star hung solely for our Son
And all around who came to share that light
Were blessed with special favors, every one.
The wise men three who followed shining star
And shepherds who adored on bended knee,
The lambs which shepherds brought Him from afar,
The cattle breathing warmth against His cheek.

Our new born son looked kindly on this lot.
He knew their cares, their woes, their endless fears.
He knew that courage got them to this spot
And shed with them their sacrificial tears.
And so he had me share with all this night
My humble gift of His birth, with the world,
The mighty and the meek, my virgin girl
While angels hovered near to guard the site.

I am Joseph,
And this is my gift

November 14, 1986

Spiritual

Repentance

My Lord
I come into this room
Wherein You sit calmly,
Resting.

It's dark,
Quiet here. I find You
Waiting, head bowed, silent,
Knowing.

I come
Like the Magdalene came
Whose many grievous sins
You heard,

Whose long
Dark hair she loosed to wipe
Her repentant tears from
Your feet.

I, too,
Now come to wash Your feet
With my own contrite tears,
My Lord,

With long remorseful strengths
I wipe them dry.

September 6, 1987

Spiritual

*"I will pour out water upon the thirsty ground, and
streams upon the dry land. I will pour out my spirit upon
your offspring."*   *Isaiah 44:3-5*

*"He who believes in me, from within him there shall flow
rivers of living water."*
                                                              John 7:38

Rivers of Life

The Living Streams are those

He sends to work His will,

Who give of selves to others

Ever in His Holy Name.

Their pathways follow

Footprints He has made

Which show the way to live,

To love, to help a friend.

Who of us has not been

touched by them and felt

Their gifts of hands upon our

troubled brows?

These flow like Living Streams

from Him.

December 7, 1991

Spiritual

There Is No Strait

There is no strait
Nor narrow path marked out,
No open shining gate,
No signs to indicate the way
Which we should take
To gain our paradise.
No lighted tunnels lead us
Through the mountains of our lives.
No promised dreams
No insured schemes
To sign or seal our fates.
We are, like all, put here
By God. Like all, imperfect lambs,
To know Him
And to follow Him
Our Shepherd
And our Friend.

September 16, 1986

Spiritual

Unborn

I hear the cries
Of the Never-to-Be,
Experience first-hand
What predestined
Purgatory will see:
The ever cries,
The never ending cries
Of babes unborn
But waiting to be:

Waiting To Be

April 10, 1986

Spiritual

People and Relationships

People and Relationships

People and Relationships

The Visitor

Who knocks
At my door, comes
To tea, to sit awhile,
To kinship share, to talk... and leaves
A friend.

August 1-13, 1987

This Flower Safety

Time was
We two could share
Our hearts, our lives, bare souls
And know that intimacy shared
Was safe.

August 1-13, 1987

People and Relationships

The Aura

Time slows

Hesitates, almost

Stops. The aura

Grows, knows

How. Knows

Somehow me

Becomes me

Is safety. Is comfort.

Is you.

Is us. Is we.

October 15, 1973

People and Relationships

Between Us

There was between us .... something .... something
No one but the other one could know:
We shared such secrets .... didn't we?
And smiled habitually over them ....

May 1, 1973

Certainty

As surely as the
Minutes tick themselves
   into tomorrow and
As silently as stars
   stare through nights of blueness
As total as compulsion
   of a mothers love
Is my certainty of
What should be
For you - for me.

January 13, 1986

People and Relationships

The Bride

As pure and
Untouched as
The unpicked morning rose
Holding tenaciously
Its one drop of dew
A precious gem
Was your beauty
That day adorned
In Ivory dress
Soft skin perfect
As the perfect
Rosebud.
Unopened
Holding back
Its gifts. Awaiting
The Perfect Moment
Of revelation,
That one precise
Instant in time
For which you
Were created.

February 12, 1986

People and Relationships

Cupids First Arrow
Age 14

He glanced my way as he passed by
Making my heart pound repeatedly
If my mother could read my thoughts
She would banish him immediately

January 17, 1943

People and Relationships

The Autumn Pruning

He carries the necessary tools outside,
Gathers them almost reverently,
Hand tools clasped in one gloved fist,
Long handled ones slung over his shoulder,
Shafts held inside a circled arm.
This is serious business, the fall pruning,
And the master craftsman is at work,
His rough blue overalls and faded denim shirt
Tight over spreading middle,
As jaw set, eyes determined, he begins,
Body bent into his work.

Slack, slack, slack... the metal ladder telescopes
Into its three sections, upward
Into the leafed regions of the great oak.
Ropes dangle through spaces between rungs
And he is testing for balance one last time.
Then he is going up, whistling as he climbs.

I think of the many autumns
I've watched this same progressive ritual
Through all the years of our togetherness
And am reminded that no matter how often
This same exercise is practiced,
His runged steps up this skinny ladder
Somehow always make me hold my breath.
By habit or impulse my hand reaches outward
To steady the ladder, but I am too far away

People and Relationships

For touching from this shadowed porch.
He does not see me watching, catching every movement.

He is up, up high,
Past the pale intricate symmetry
Of the robin's deserted, sadly empty, summer nest,
His perfect head disappearing
Into the changing leaf colors.

Moments pass... then a slow... almost musical...
Thunk... thunk... thunk...
As the long-handled limb trimmer
Follows the dictates of its master's plan.
And branches part, pause, shake, give, come
Floating down, stems and leaves flattening
Against air, fan into it, down, and flop
Softly onto ground from unexpected heights
And in delicate patterns, fall.

They form a slowly widening colored collar
Against the great oak's long brown neck.
Each year this tender ritual is repeated:
As the King pulls pins to loose the Queen's held tresses,
The Queen bestows her jeweled locks of hair.

August 30, 1987

People and Relationships

The Christmas Year

Tis the day after Christmas
And all through the house
A strange quietness prevails
Over even my spouse.
Empty stockings hang limp
Near the Christmas tree frayed
And ribbons lie torn
With their bows disarrayed.
A few chosen presents
Lie under the tree
In lop-sided balance
For late comers to see.
Mama is splayed out
In her last years pajama.
Papa mutely surveys
The room's wild panorama
Of cardboard, torn paper
And mistletoe jaded,
Tarnished tinsel and tissue
And Christmas tree faded.
They eye one another
And hope they'll be blessed
With a year full of days
To clean up the mess.

December 25, 1977

People and Relationships

Early Morning Kiss

To the incredible quiet
Just before dawn
There is no comparison:
With no machinery humming,
No movement save the
Gentle breath of light wind,
The consoling sound of early birds'
Softly fluttering wing, the night
Insects cacophony settling down
For day.   No people talk.
Without distraction
Earth rests her Giant Rest.
Night creatures close in upon
Themselves. Before the cock crows,
Revelers, just now asleep from
Their carousals, are forced
Not to face the day
Lest they die from the
Pain of so much
Beauty missed.
This quiet time, I kiss.

April 1984

People and Relationships

Great Granny's Face

Her muted days are measured now
By the wrinkles in her face
All rutted pathways
Of travels she has known:
Some blessed, some cursed,
But none she would carelessly erase.
They stand as proof,
As proving of her worth –
Like tithings to the church,
The marks she'd paid her dues.

May 25, 1986

People and Relationships

Guilt

Careful
We must not tell anyone
About the Failures
The rattling
Skeletons
Hiding in bare closets
The keyholes stopped
With pinking
Bubblegum
Hardening
Witness to the necessity for
Utter secrecy
In matters of
Mommy.

February 3, 1986

(After reading "Mommy Dearest) – Key-
hole shaped.

People and Relationships

La Cloche de Grandmere
(Grandmother's Bell)

Down the dark hallway
Back to the stair
Hung the old keeper
La cloche de grandmere

Ringing in birth
Tolling out death
Leading the living
And laying to rest

Calling to mealtimes
Three times a dayThe diligent
gardner,
And children from play

Old faithful ringer,
We called it those years,
Took some living hand
To toll its call clear

Over the hedges
And back to the barn
On every occasion
Of joy or alarm

And love of its ringer
Behind every note
Brought our attention
Up from the remote

For loving hands
Ring salient calls
Bringing hearts closer
But best of all:

Closer to home
To whats important:
Life and the living of
Love as it quotient.

July 16, 1970

People and Relationships

Lady Light

Martha Ellen

Ebony fathoms
Embracing sparks of light,
Brownish tips
Changing, reflectively
Sometimes to yellow:
Modifying what is.
A cacophony of
Intelligence searching
Finding
Murmuring truths
Opening doors
experimentally
To safes.
Daring to close them.
Confronting disparity,
Reconciling.
Past my own hopes.
A streaking blue energy
Flashing Royalty,
A Green Heavy Lovely Peopled valley.

October 12, 1982

People and Relationships

Love in My Hospital Room

Watching the city come awake
That morning from my hospital window
Reminded me of our love awakening:

Slowly at first, with a dim light
Here - and - there. And later,
With the dawn, the whole world came
alive,
Clean with the excitement of new day,
Rich with the promise of new light.
All the fog lifted —
And how brightly shone the sun!

March 15, 1974

People and Relationships

Miss Junior High

Hello
Miss Junior High:
Diminutive She
Somehow delicately
Awkward
Gangling of Girl.
Being surely woman;
Not yet however
Knowing Lithe,
But trying
Desperately to become.
Using funky haircuts,
Wearing high heels
On unsure feet
To help balance
A tightrope walk
Between then and there.
A reverse echo
Of her future self
All Echoes of her past
Rolled into one
Immediate Imperative
Present.

December 19, 1985

People and Relationships

Naivete

To Catherine

In Infinity
You remain the noblest
Of noble. You are.
You laugh, love, sigh,
Dip honey. Tell truths.
Reality abides pure mirth,
Spins silver song
On golden thread.
Your smile
Knows no artifice.
All is revealed
Through your eyes
Which defy deception.
The uncurtained soul
Triumphs in you.
In you.

May 20, 1977

People and Relationships

Oh, Suzanne
(To the Poet's Daughter)

Calm certainty
In search of
Ultimate Importances.
A bundle of regal beauty
With a thoughtful face
Holding a cold world
In soft warm hands
Weighing validity against false-
hood
Testing for flaws
All things suspect.
Superb direction
Setting the stage
For grand climaxes,
Glamour playing
Five card stud
Against nurture
In a juggling
Hands-on search for fulfillment.
Romantic intelligence
Dressed in Midnight blue
Satin and lace, Magically
Managing to make
All things end
Somehow
FinallyBalanced.

December 2, 1985

People and Relationships

Old Grievances

The huddled cabin by the sea is
                    weather worn,
With aged grey plankings sanded
                    by the wind.
The whole place: house, reeds,
                    dunes, and tree,
All lean northward, into safety
                    from the sea,
As though in fear cringed
                    prisoners
At the wall who would be shot
                    at dawn,
But stay, they know must stay,
                    to face the end.

Inside the hut, a fire sparks,
                    draws air,
The cat claws at the door to
                    be let in.
Repeated scratchings on the
                    wood
Make rasping sounds, nerve raking
                    sounds, and
Through stretched years the old,
                    raw plank
Is sanded smooth there, bare
                    in naked cold,
Where she knocked often, knocked
                    to be let in,
And often wounded painted wood.
Upstairs, a shutter loosed of nail
                    is hanging
In the wind, is banged, and
                    banged again,
Betraying thoughts I had it nailed.

People and Relationships

But it's undone again and will
                    remain so,
Where it hangs, color chipped,
                    in chipping wind.

Outside, the sea casts in, and out,
                    against the sand,
And smooths old stones, once jagged,
                    once betrayed
By chance and old gods' whims,

Rattling tiny ones into ever
                    smaller bits
Of nothingness until they sift back
                    smaller,
Smaller, sift to sand.   And sit
                    there in
Inverterate redundancy, and by millions
                    scream at me.
Mocking!   Mocking Me!

In all the world, the house,

Inside and out, the door,
        are failed reprieves, by scores,
Solutions never loosed, resolved,

Where old undoings fluttered,
                    festered long,
Are now washed clean of stain,
                    by sand and sea,
But they remain, are blown by
                    wind and rattle still.
The day sun sets dies slowly
                    on this beach.

28 October 1987

103

People and Relationships

On Being Locked Out

Through the smokescreen

Of immediate pain

I search the billowed

Corners

Looking for some obscure tear, one

Iota of redeeming meaning,

Some hidden new lesson

I might (this late?)

Perhaps have missed.

However scrupulous

My private,

Probing search,

It evades me -

Until finally, hurt

And bitterness removed,

I find it

Hiding there

Impersonating

My teacher.

January 29, 1986

People and Relationships

Pathways Taken

Fine traceries etched time
Upon the smooth skin of her face
Mementoes all of her nobility –
A reaching into and out of rhyme
Beyond the wedding of her soul and mind.

October 1980

Proximity

As ivy growing up a tree,
I cling as close to thee
And hide thy nakedness;
In green abundance dress
Thy brittle bark. I
Slowly stretch myself
Thy farthest reach,
Until we are as one as
They, the ivy and the tree.

February 20, 1976

People and Relationships

Rose Footnote

Faded
Old, Sweet,
Breath Of rose slipped
Pressed from between pages
Of her book
Lacing memories
And momentous magic of
Some remembered past.
Was that once fair bud
So fragrance graced
Her talisman,
Or does that marking
Grace the pages
Of her song?

April 3, 1986

People and Relationships

San Luis Obisbo
October 13, 1983 - at Pismo Beach

Remember...
When after supper
That cool fall evening
We walked sweaterless hand in hand
Through scattered eucalyptus
To the pebbled sandy beach...
To watch the water turquoised blue
As rippling waves
Washed gently in,
Then out again
Across the rocky agate shore...
We stood breathlessly, arms linked,
Statued in silent awe
To watch the sunset
Orange up our sky...
The seagulls flew for us...
  they dipped and hovered almost on command
And drew the wind which chilled us through.
Smiling, we wrapped one the other
In encircling arms.
We both had known
It was too cool
To be outdoors without sweaters.

September 17, 1986

People and Relationships

She Was Pastels

She was pastels
Against soft white
A seafoam green
Indian Beaded flower
Of immutable presence
Gossamer Spirited,
Winged whenever necessary
To escape
Through flung windows,
Her own fallibility
Searching indelibility:
Those known delicate
But deliberate inkings
Strict from
A pale, pale pen.

April 8, 1986

People and Relationships

To Allison

You came to me

A shy bundle

Grown under my heart;

A sprinkle of gold-red hair

Sucking its thumb,

Asking nothing save love ...

Giving so much more:

A tender trustfulness,

A carefully careless

Certainty of right,

Fierce loyalty,

Simple, gracious Love.

For what more

Could one ask

In a child?

April 20, 1982

People and Relationships

Toby Boy

I have a secret playing place
Where no one else can be,
A cozy hidden corner mine
Behind big chair in the library.

No other one will I let in
To share that private space.
It's all mine and I am its,
My palace hiding place.

There are such things that go on there
No other would believe---
Wars with soldiers and Indians too,
Every game I can conceive.

The library books look down from shelves
Too high for me to see
And wish they knew what's going on
In my little three-by-three.

I'll tell you what it is in there
That keeps me busy bee---
Besides my soldiers and their wars,
It's that no one else can see.

March 28, 1968

110

People and Relationships

Two Women

Let's be friends again
Like when we were girls.
Let's be women together
Washing our hair
Trading beauty secrets
And recipes. Let's
Take walks in the woods
On brisk days in autumn.
Watch the leaves fall.
The golden leaves of change
Signal our changes.
Let's compare notes
On husbands, Children, menus,
Pathways once chosen
- And those not taken.
Let's revive old memories
We've each had tucked away
For later use. Now is the time
To be our old young selves again
At a new place that is
Solely womanhoods.
Sharing secret places of the heart
Which none but us can know.
Especially in the autumn.

August 9, 1985

The Undoing

It irritates me when

I see him walking 'round

Or sitting down as

Though that's all

There is in life to do:

Not merely a waste, but

A taking of space.

Just sitting. Not knitting,

Nor whittling, nor spittling.

Just sitting. Not doing,

Simply <u>undoing.</u>

Can that be the irritant

I find it difficult

To put my finger on?

The Un-Doing???

October 24, 1985

People and Relationships

?Who Is There?

You don't hear because

 you don't listen.

You don't see because

 you don't look.

What is it you don't hear,

You don't see

Whom?

April 16, 1986

113

People and Relationships

Within Your Eyes

Faith:
> For years I searched,
> My eyes seeking yours, always seeking,
> Not knowing where
> Nor how we'd meet,
> Not quite sure I'd ever really find you.
> But you are here
> And it was faith
> Which brought you to me.

Hope:
> And yet
> It was the sure determination
> Of that search, the almost
> Certainty
> You'd one day come
> Which demanded I wait for you,
> And that was hope.

Love:
> Beloved, together now
> Our constant love will strengthen all our rooms,
> Brighten all our vistas,
> Color all our dreams, and
> Make bearable our passages.
> And Love, from today forevermore,
> Whenever I approach our gate
> Or open our front door
> I'll know it is for you I've searched,
> It is for you I long
> And it is within your eyes
> I find myself.

Lee Olivier Cleghorn,

On the occasion of the wedding of Allison
Cavalier and Tony Whitehead, my children.
September 4, 1993

Death and Loss

Death and Loss

Death and Loss

On Dying

QUESTIONER: Must I go now?

ANGEL: Yes, the time has come.

QUESTIONER: But I'm not prepared! The time has been so short!

ANGEL: But you are prepared. You have been aimed in this direction since the day you were born.

QUESTIONER: I have?....(Pause)....Yes, I know that's true...
...and yet....

ANGEL: Come. We must go. The hour is here.

QUESTIONER: ....And yet....(Pause)....I wish to stay.

ANGEL: Have you not had enough, of struggle, of pain?

QUESTIONER: But not enough of joy!

ANGEL: Life was not made for joy. Your joy has been your strength. Your strength has been your life.

QUESTIONER: It has been a struggle....... With more defeat than victory.

ANGEL: All..... the struggle, the pain, the strife, the strength....and, yes, the courage.... have been your victory.

QUESTIONER: Then I have lived well?

ANGEL: You have lived well.

QUESTIONER: It was not easy.

ANGEL: EASY? ...... Think. .... Was it _not_ easy?

Death and Loss

QUESTIONER: Perhaps it was. But this....this going into

      death .... the unknown....is strange to me.

ANGEL: That is why I am here.

QUESTIONER: To reassure me?

ANGEL: .....And to guide you....

QUESTIONER: To what?

ANGEL: Through the darkness.... to the light.

QUESTIONER: It is light!

ANGEL: There is nothing else.

QUESTIONER: I see nothing else. But yes, ...there is some

      darkness. There!

ANGEL: Take my hand.

QUESTIONER: Oh!! ....(Pause)....The light increases!

ANGEL: Yes.

QUESTIONER: ....And yet increases...... Surely!

ANGEL: Yes.

QUESTIONER: Stay with me!

ANGEL: Yes.

  (Long Pause)

QUESTIONER: (Softly).......Oooohhhhh!

ANGEL: You see....... we're here!

January 16, 1976

118

Death and Loss

Crying Is the Willow

Someone there is
Who stands alone
Beneath the willows
Waiting, softly cries;
Rain and tears commingle
In the weeping willows --
Wet leaves fall like teardrops
On the cheek of air,
Like teardrops on cheek so fair
Of one who is standing there
Crying in the Willow
Crying in the Willow

Crying is the Willow.

May 10, 1986

119

Death and Loss

The Alcoholic

The lure of amber
Made slipping in
Through that narrow neck
Past unrecrossable lip
Easy. Strange how
From inside that cylindrical
Glass beckoned luring
Magical strengths.
Auras. Janus
Promising new wisdoms,
Enticing solutions
To increasingly painful
Misgivings. Damnation
Masked as salvation
Once the amber liquid ran
Low. Treachery
Where all former promises
Were broken
As certainly as
They never existed.

January 17, 1986

Death and Loss

The Funeral

The organist is playing "Panis Angelicus"
While the choir sings.
Light filters through colored glass
From the round East window
So I know it must be morning.

The light rays reveal dust particles
Floating in a columnar tube
To rest on the wooden coffin
Centered on the aisle-close altar.
Dust at once reminds me, defines me.

The Priest in his brocaded robe
Faces the people who wait
For the music to end, for him to speak.
His hands hold the thurible...
Its thin chain delicately clicks, clicks.

Beside him stands an altar boy
Dressed in black cassock, white surplice,
Looking somber and dignified, eyes downcast.
He could be my brother, but isn't.

My brother once stood so
When I married in this same church
But he has aged, is old, grey.
The soloist is singing now, alone.

Her perfect voice cuts through incensed air
Which swirls, puffs, rises up above my coffin.
She sings "Panis Angelicus"
Just like I always wanted.

September 1, 1987

Death and Loss

Grief

The quickened, eager
   footstep gone
The pulse has slowed
The soul feels dead
A stooped shadow walks
   morose instead.
That once joyous face
   looks pinched
No longer smiles:
For that bent figure
Shows its mourning now.
All else is small
Compared to that
For which she lived
There are no songs
No notes to play
To drown the awful
Sounds of grief
No poetry exists.

October 2, 1973

Death and Loss

On the Explosion of Challenger

Our nation mourns
New tragedy today
Mourning now new death
Nipping at Our Stars:
Seven Bold Bright Stars
Zooming through
Crisp blue space
Toward unforeseen
Destinies. A flash.
Quick. One wishes
To reach out a hand -
Slow it - Stop it.
A grasp through space,
To stop what
Already is a cloud
Of mercy covering all.

A long hard gasp
Escapes the silence.
The Seven Darers:
The strongest, bravest Those,
Courageous enough
To try the space
Surmount the risk of Challenge
At the risk of life
Are sprinkled there permanently
Like Stars shot
Through Heavens,
Where they
Wished
To Be.

January 28, 1986

Death and Loss

Without You Things Are Desolate

I wanted music last summer
But all I got was dead
Cold silence on a hot beach
With dry tangled sandy hair
Scratching my wet face.
Without you things are desolate

I wanted poetry last summer
But all I got was grey rain
Along a bleak deserted street
In the city - with no soft
Place to lay my head.
Without you things are desolate

I wanted song last summer
But all I got was a bare harsh
Abandoned piece of land
With an empty cabin and
   A loose door -
And no one there to fix it.
Without you things are desolate

August 9, 1985

Death and Loss

Rest Well Old Soldier
(On the death of the Poet's Father)

Rest well, old soldier.
In memory of your faithful life,
Take peace.
Your soul, reborn,
Arises from this awful grief
  Clasping to its breast
  Release.
Into new dawns awake
  refreshed.
Thy scaffold has been
  Life itself
Its ropes and beams
  your scourges.
How could you not
  expect relief?
Take heart and rest.
Heaven has been earned.
All group with all
  to comfort thee.
Give up the struggle
And in giving up, take peace
For that reward is here
Your time is now eternal.

February 15, 1974

125

Death and Loss

Song to Jess

On those late September days, Jess
When twilight comes earlier
To bring the purple sky
Of night, and its thin
Silver slice of moon is bright
We'll think of you,
Of all your gentle
Husbandry and quiet ways
And fatherliness to us.

Each whispered evening
Hush in late September, Jess
With silvered slice of moon
In purple dress
We'll think of you again...
... with thankfulness.

We loved you, Jess.

September 30, 1992

Death and Loss

Coming Into Grief

One blackbird flying stark
against a cold grey sky--
as we glide our steel grey car
along grey asphalt drive

While I

While I

Weep tears, oh, fear grey tears
against unwitting cheek
from cold grey eyes
like slow incessant rain
from these low clouded skies.

We know where we go, we cry
but he knows not, nor why.
Dark silhouette against that sky,
he flies his heart intact--

Not I

Not I

January 9, 1987

Death and Loss

That Long Way Home

That last long walk from the cemetery
Our trudging out and home
Begins at the church. The slow ingress
And out following her casket,
I now carrying her cross.
Her last attempts at peace now futile,
Now mine her futility.

The small ebony and silver crucifix
Heavies my hand. I hold it up before me
For all to see and I follow her in black.
I walk the long aisle of her church
Through many generations,
This place the final testimony to her life.

The organist plays her hymnal tribute
As sunlight pours through tall stained glass.
Her Monsignor presses words as seals
Upon the foreheads of her mourners,
Follows her impressioned footsteps
Through our lives and Christ's.
Oh she is gone. Is gone...
Her spirit even now rises, rises...
Is raised up. Walks through golden portals
While mournful eyes watch through incensed air.

In drawn out gasps we cry our loss.
One slow telling bell is tolled,
My cried out soul thus further wrung.

That Long Way Home.

October 1987

128

Death and Loss

To Mother on Her Birthday
July 24, 1988

Mama
Has it really been almost a year
Since you went on
Leaving me, the eldest now
Oh, so alone?

When I
Think of you
I still see those thin-skinned
bony hands
knuckles twisted,
See those
rough skinned hands,
with serrated nails,
fingers trembling.

Trying
to hold on against
even your own will,
belying your desire to go.

The ever, ever
arching curve to shoulders
which proved
bones do after all
give way
to the pull, pull
downward pull of gravity

"Stand straight, Sister.

I also see
those mincing
feet on their thin legs
which nevertheless managed
to get you up
every morning,
despite all contrary predictions,
even to the last day
when they finally gave way.

And you were so strong
you tiny worn thing.

July 20, 1988

129